ROGUES AND VILLAINS

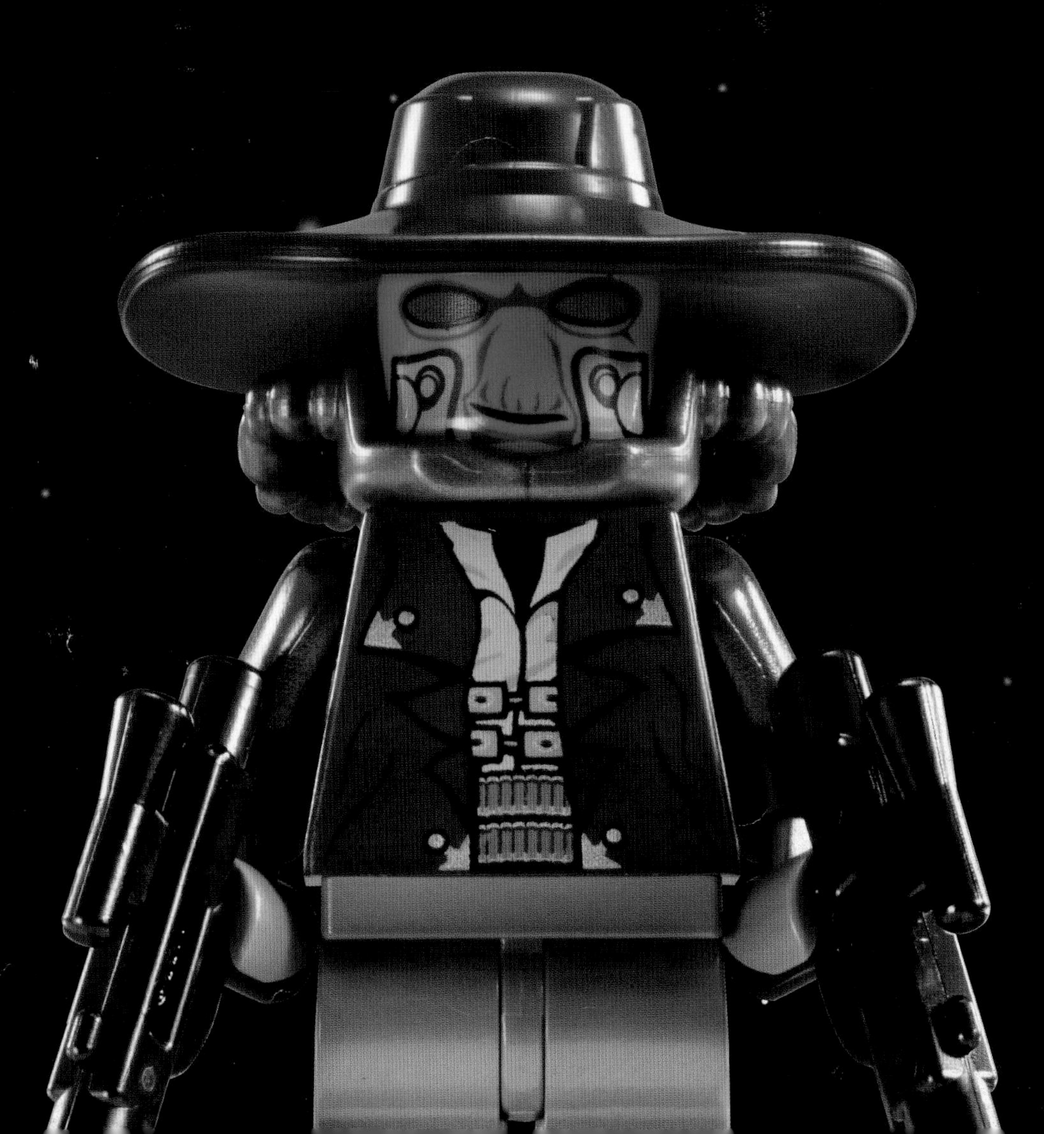

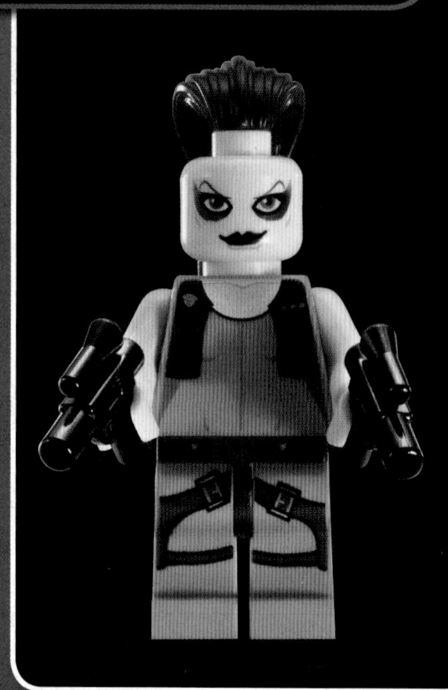

INTRODUCTION

Bounty hunters and villains plague the LEGO® *Star Wars* galaxy. Find out about this incredible bunch of minifigures—from the greedy Jabba the Hutt to the mysterious B'omarr Monk.

HOW TO USE THIS BOOK

These amazing minifigures are ordered according to the *Star Wars®* property in which they first appeared or mostly featured. Tabs at the top of each page indicate which properties this minifgure appears in. As most Star Wars characters appear in the Expanded Universe, that tab is highlighted only if a minifigure appears in an EU set. The Clone Wars tab has not been highlighted if the character has a separate Clone Wars minifigure.

This book also includes variants of featured minifigures, which are the same character, but have some modifications that make them different in some way.

Contents

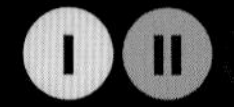

This tricky Toydarian junk dealer is a tough minifigure to get hold of! Watto first appeared in a single set in 2001, Watto's Junkyard (set 7186), and was not seen again—until he resurfaced in 2011 with a new look. As he is constantly in flight, Watto's minifigure has a translucent stand to raise him above the dusty earth of Tatooine.

STAR VARIANT

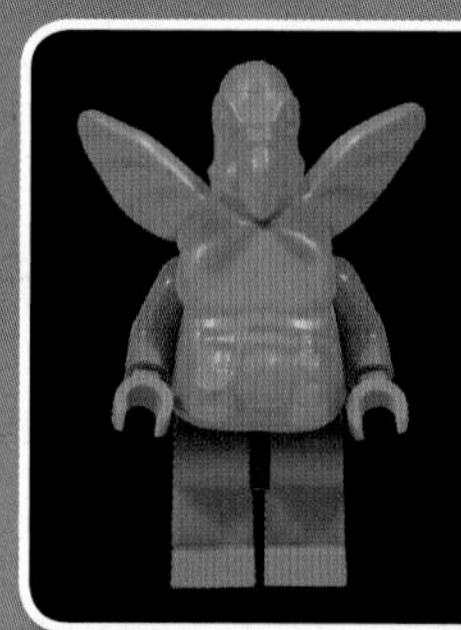

Blue Watto

The original variant of winged Watto is not one for details—he has a plain blue head and torso piece with no printing on it. Underneath that is a plain tan torso piece. This variant is rare, appearing in only one 2001 set: Watto's Junkyard (set 7186).

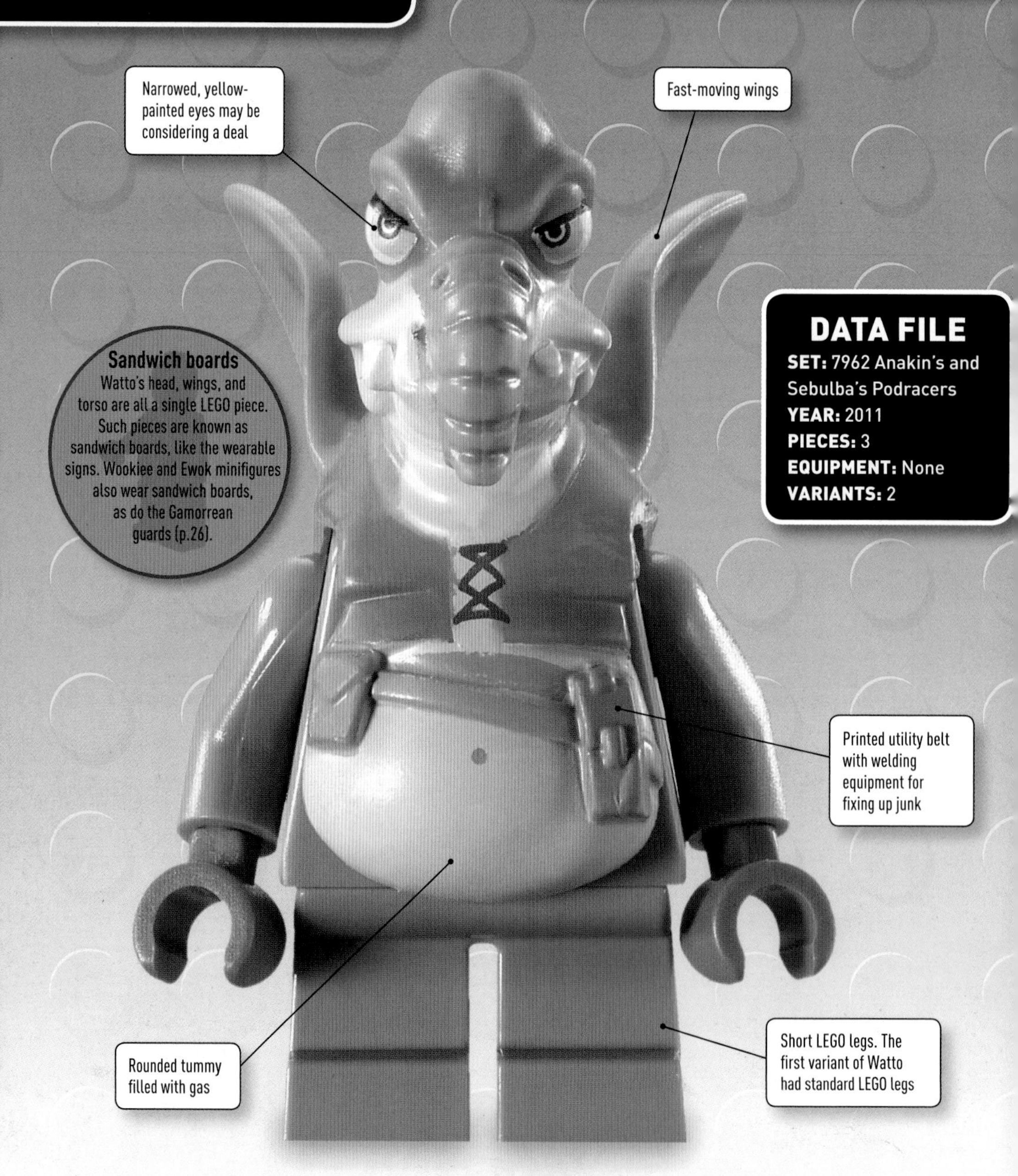

Sandwich boards

Watto's head, wings, and torso are all a single LEGO piece. Such pieces are known as sandwich boards, like the wearable signs. Wookiee and Ewok minifigures also wear sandwich boards, as do the Gamorrean guards (p.26).

DATA FILE

SET: 7962 Anakin's and Sebulba's Podracers
YEAR: 2011
PIECES: 3
EQUIPMENT: None
VARIANTS: 2

Sebulba
PODRACER PILOT

Dangerous Dug Sebulba is the arch rival of Anakin Skywalker and one of the most successful Podracers on Tatooine—mostly through his ruthless rule-breaking. He made his minifigure debut in 1999 at the helm of his imposing orange Pod packed with deadly weapons, and reemerged in 2011 clad in a flashy leather race outfit.

Anakin's and Sebulba's Podracers (set 7962)

Sebulba's Podracer in the Anakin's and Sebulba's Podracers set is built to intimidate. Not only is it bigger than his opponents' Podracers, but it also has a bunch of illegal weapons—some hidden—for sabotage purposes during the race.

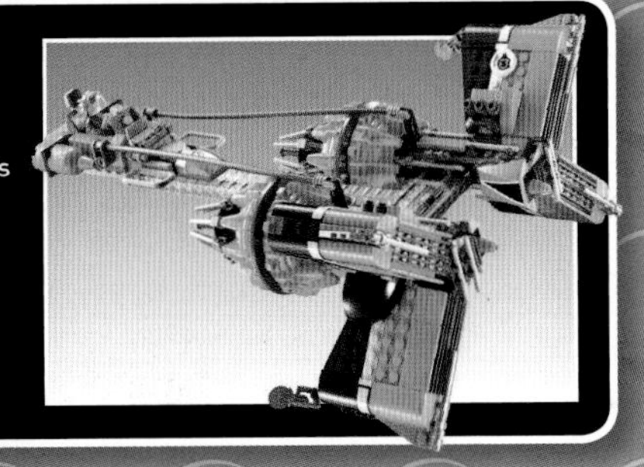

STAR VARIANT

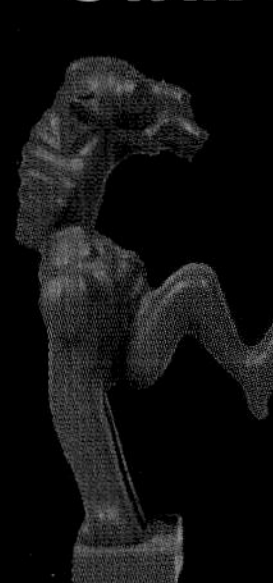

Static Sebulba
The original Sebulba is all one LEGO piece and has no movement capabilities, making it an unusual minifigure. This variant is rare—it is exclusive to the 2001 set, Mos Espa Podrace (set 7171).

Racing cap with goggles

Sebulba's head and body are one LEGO piece, but his arms are removeable

Sebulba has adapted his hind limbs to steer his Podracer

Sebulba walks on his arms. They are moveable on the 2011 redesign

Tight leg straps wind around Sebulba's hands

DATA FILE

SET: 7962 Anakin's and Sebulba's Podracers
YEAR: 2011
PIECES: 3
EQUIPMENT: None
VARIANTS: 2

Aldar Beedo

PODRACER PILOT

This mercenary minifigure has accepted payment for taking down his racing rival Sebulba during the Boonta Eve Classic Podrace. Can Aldar Beedo complete his task? His pretty impressive Podracer appears in the 2001 LEGO set Watto's Junkyard (set 7186) along with the latest variant of his lanky Glymphid minifigure.

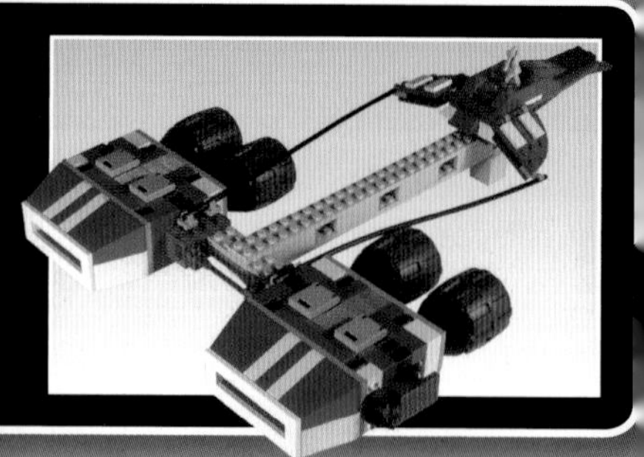

Watto's Junkyard (set 7186)
The 2001 variant of Aldar Beedo is exclusively featured in Watto's Junkyard. His impressive Podracer is a *Mark IV* Flat-Twin Turbojet model with huge engines and afterburners. Beedo fits inside the pod.

This Podracer clearly isn't too worried about safety—he isn't wearing a flight helmet! But Beedo's original variant wears a brown helmet

Elongated Glymphid snout

Glymphids have suction cups on their fingertips

The LEGO Group created Aldar Beedo's long, thin minifigure mold especially for him

Stand fits into the cockpit of Beedo's Podracer. It is not removeable from his body

STAR VARIANT

Older Aldar
This variant of Aldar Beedo appears in the *Star Wars* Podracing Bucket (set 7159), in a simplified version of Beedo's Podracer. The minifigure has no unique LEGO pieces and his body is mostly made up of parts from battle droid minifigures.

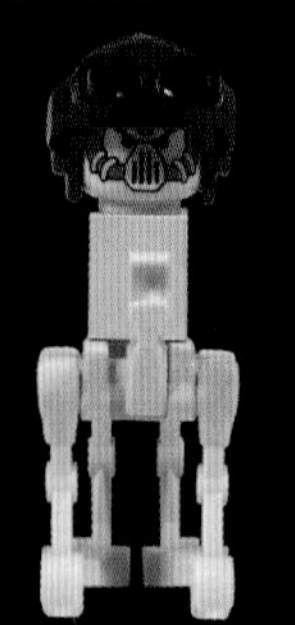

DATA FILE

SET: 7186 Watto's Junkyard
YEAR: 2001
PIECES: 1
EQUIPMENT: None
VARIANTS: 2

One piece
Aldar Beedo is one of the few LEGO minifigures to be made from a single LEGO piece. The original variant of Beedo's Podracing rival Sebulba (p.7) is the only other single-piece minifigure in the LEGO *Star Wars* theme.

Multitasking minifigure Gasgano likes to keep his Podracing competitors at arm's length! He employs his many LEGO arms to pilot his Podracer at great speeds and takes second place in the Boonta Eve Classic. Blink and you will miss him, as the minifigure only appears in one LEGO *Star Wars* set.

Mos Espa Podrace (set 7171)
Watch out for Gasgano in this 1999 LEGO set—he is one of the fastest Podracers on the track! His exclusive minifigure can reach enormous speeds in his powerful LEGO Podracer thanks to anti-turbulence vanes that move as the craft races for the finish line of the Boonta Eve Classic.

This light gray LEGO helmet is popular on the Podracing circuit—young Podracer Anakin Skywalker also wears it

Gasgano's white head with large alien eyes and a driven stare is unique to his minifigure

Gasgano's arms
In Episode I, Gasgano has six arms, but his LEGO minifigure only has four! Two of Gasgano's arms work the foot pedals of his Podracer during a race and can't be seen—this may be why his minifigure has just four arms.

These arm pieces feature on many droid minifigures in LEGO *Star Wars*

Gasgano is the only LEGO minifigure to feature this piece. It is often part of a chain saw tool in other sets

DATA FILE
SET: 7171 Mos Espa Podrace
YEAR: 1999
PIECES: 8
EQUIPMENT: None
VARIANTS: 1

Tusken Raider
DESERT DWELLER

This fearsome Tusken Raider is part of a fierce nomadic species native to Tatooine. The mysterious minifigure can move almost invisibly through dusty desert dunes dressed in his desert-colored sandshroud. His unique LEGO head and torso pieces are adapted to help him survive in intense heat.

Desert details
The Tusken's sandshroud and crossed utility belt are also printed on the back of his unique torso piece.

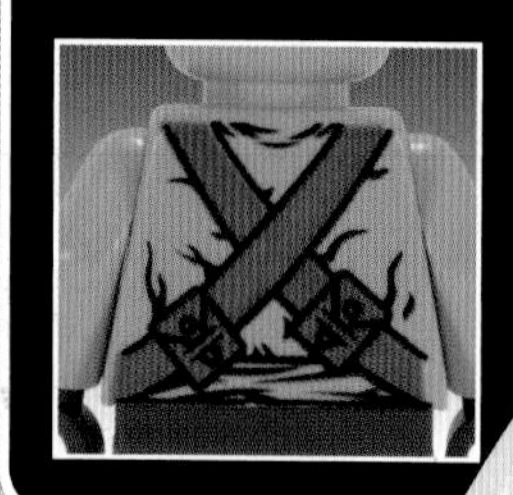

Eye goggles offer protection from the fierce desert sun

Bandaged face mask on this unique head piece has an open mouth to facilitate breathing

This moisture trap humidifies the dry desert air before the Tusken breathes it in

The Tusken Raider's LEGO torso piece is unique. It is covered in rags to protect him from sand and conserve moisture

Some Tusken Raider minifigures have these tan hips, but most have appeared with gray hips

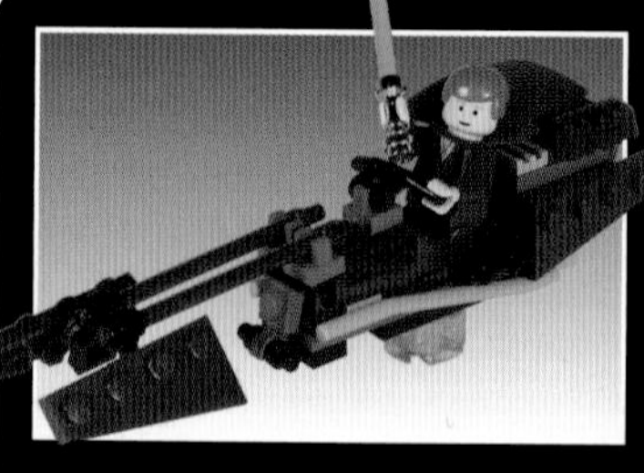

Tusken Raider Encounter (set 7113)
The Tusken Raider is exclusive to this set, which contains two of the minifigures. The Tuskens have captured Anakin's mother, Shmi. When an enraged Anakin discovers their primitive camp on his swoop bike, it can only mean trouble.

DATA FILE
SET: 7113 Tusken Raider Encounter
YEAR: 2002
PIECES: 3
EQUIPMENT: Projectile rifle
VARIANTS: 1

Jabba The Hutt

INTERGALACTIC GANGSTER

Jabba the Hutt is a slimy, green crime lord who orchestrates shady schemes across the LEGO *Star Wars* galaxy. The vile villain's head-and-torso piece is a unique LEGO mold. It is almost impossible to miss Jabba's enormous slug-like minifigure—even though he only comes in two LEGO sets.

Jabba's Palace (set 4480)
Jabba sits on a raised throne in his royal palace, where he keeps an eye on his slave, Princess Leia. There is a sneaky trapdoor beneath the throne, which Jabba can open to dispose of anyone who is silly enough to get on his nerves!

DATA FILE
SET: 4480 Jabba's Palace
YEAR: 2003
PIECES: 3
EQUIPMENT: None
VARIANTS: 1

Facial features are defined by the unique mold, not by any printed detail

Jabba's sand-green coloring matches the skin tone of his Gamorrean guards

Although Jabba's head and torso is a single LEGO piece, the arms are poseable

Jabba's favorite snack is a slimy gorg. LEGO gorgs are actually transparent green frog pieces

Tail tales
Jabba's minifigure requires some assembly: His slimy tail comes in two pieces that clip together. The end piece is also used for the tail of Obi-Wan's varactyl, Boga, and for the tails of the dewback creatures of Tatooine.

Rotta The Hutt
JABBA'S SON

Often referred to as "the Huttlet," Rotta is the slimy, green son of Jabba the Hutt. Poor Rotta has been captured by the Separatists. Can Anakin Skywalker and Ahsoka Tano rescue him and return him to his worried father? The Jedi will have to search hard for Rotta's small minifigure, as he only comes in two LEGO sets.

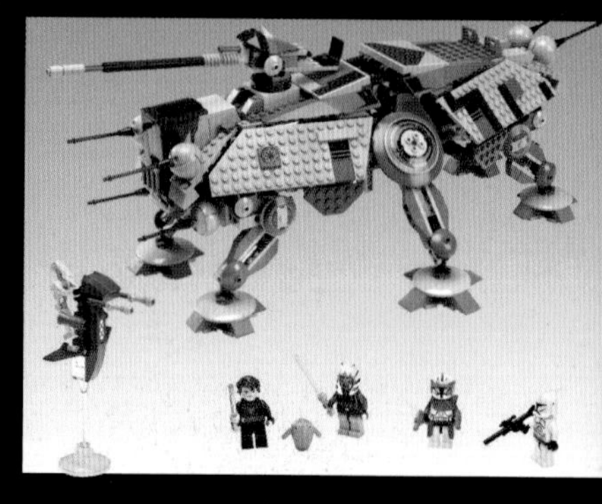

AT-TE Walker (set 7675)
Rotta makes his first LEGO appearance in the 2008 set AT-TE Walker. Jabba's young son is in good LEGO hands when he is rescued by the Jedi. Anakin and Ahsoka are joined by two clone troopers and an enormous AT-TE walker—together they have no trouble defeating the battle droid on his flying STAP.

DATA FILE
SET: 7675 AT-TE Walker
YEAR: 2008
PIECES: 3
EQUIPMENT: None
VARIANTS: 1

Rotta's mold
Rotta's minifigure is built from three unique, sand-green LEGO pieces. The two arm pieces clip into the head and body piece, which is a unique mold, made especially for this minifigure.

Rotta may not be much use on the battlefield, but Ahsoka thinks he is cute!

Like most Clone Wars minifigures, Rotta has painted eyes

Although he is small now, one day Rotta might grow up to be as large as his father Jabba (p. 11)

Rotta has a hollow circle in the base of his minifigure so he can be clipped onto a regular minifigure's hand

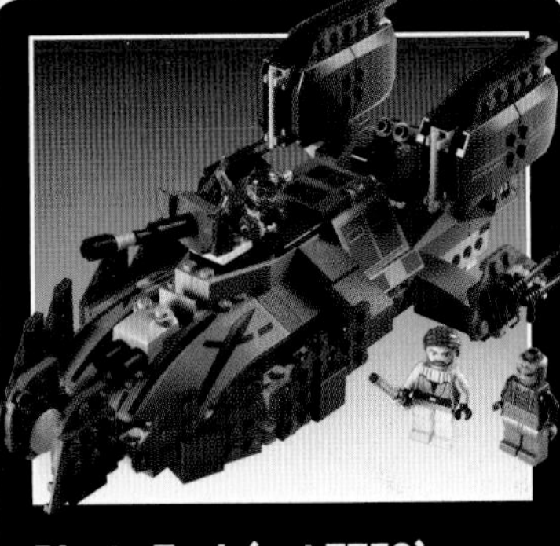

Pirate Tank (set 7753)

Hondo is the gunner on board the pirate tank in this set. The tank is equipped with flick-fire missiles and a huge blaster cannon. Hondo and his gang of pirates are on a mission to kidnap Obi-Wan—the Jedi Master will fetch a good ransom!

Hondo Ohnaka is the f
leader of a gang of Weequa
pirates. His minifigure wea
mismatched clothes, a bla
bandana, and green-eyed g
—items he has scavenged
many journeys. Hondo only
in one LEGO set, but he an
pilfering gang are always
new ways to make a quic

Black bandana is also worn by the Weequay bounty hunter Shahan Alama (p.17)

Hondo's unique head is printed with goggles and Weequay skin

Shoulder epaulets show all the other pirates who's in charge

Epaulet
The LEGO epaulet shoulder piece is worn by several minifigures across other LEGO themes, including pirates and soldiers. In LEGO *Star Wars*, however, only two minifigures wear epaulets: Hondo and Embo (p.19).

Torso is printed with an elaborate jacket, which Hondo wears over a ragged white shirt. Hondo thinks the jacket gives him a sense of grandeur

Only two other LEGO *Star Wars* minifigures have dark red arm pieces: Commander Fox and Chancellor Palpatine

DATA FILE

SET: 7753 Pirate Tank
YEAR: 2009
PIECES: 5
EQUIPMENT: Spear gun
VARIANTS: 1

Turk Falso
DANGEROUS PIRATE

Turk Falso is a tough Weequay criminal. His minifigure is second-in-command in Hondo Ohnaka's pirate gang, and he wears clothes suitable for a pirate's life of planet hopping and petty thieving. Turk searches for Jedi minifigures to hold for ransom, but he's also out to double-cross his fellow pirates. Luckily for everyone, this rotten pirate only appears in one set.

Pirate ponytail
Turk's black ponytail is printed on the back of his head—and continues down the back of his torso.

DATA FILE

SET: 7753 Pirate Tank
YEAR: 2009
PIECES: 3
EQUIPMENT: Cutlass, twin pistols
VARIANTS: 1

Unique head piece is printed with Turk's leathery Weequay face

Turk's headband wraps all the way round the head piece and ties up at the back

Turk is the only minifigure in the LEGO *Star Wars* theme with dark green arms

Unique torso is printed on both sides with Turk's tattered clothing and weapon harness

Turk carries a pair of ancient pistols. The same LEGO pistols are used for the 2007 destroyer droid

Man of weapons
Turk wields many weapons in his crime-filled life. He uses this dark bluish-gray cutlass to threaten Jedi hostages.

Cad Bane

FEARSOME BOUNTY HUNTER

Cad Bane is a bounty hunter like no other, so it is fitting that his minifigure is the same. Wearing a unique hat and torso, Cad's blue-skinned minifigure wears a specially designed breathing apparatus and wields the villain's trademark twin blasters. He plots, schemes, and attacks the Jedi in two LEGO sets.

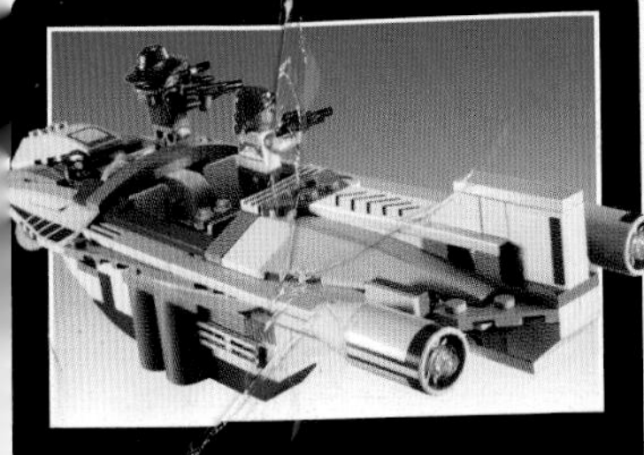

Cad Bane's Speeder (set 8128)

Cad Bane pilots a sleek speeder when he needs to make a quick getaway. The ship can fit six minifigures, including the pirate Shahan Alama (pictured)—and it has a secret compartment for contraband!

With his wide-brimmed hat, Cad thinks of himself as a space cowboy

Cad is a Duros, who all have blue skin and red eyes

Cad is prepared for any situation. He even wears a breathing apparatus just in case!

Unique torso is printed with Cad's tattered brown jacket, under which he conceals a utility belt and lots of ammunition

Cad wears rocket boots so he can fly for short distances

DATA FILE

SET: 8128 Cad Bane's Speeder
YEAR: 2010
PIECES: 5
EQUIPMENT: Breathing apparatus, twin blasters
VARIANTS: 1

Aurra Sing
RELENTLESS BOUNTY HUNTER

Ruthless bounty hunter Aurra Sing will stop at nothing to get her prize. Her fearless minifigure is dressed in an orange jumpsuit laden with weapons, but wears no armor! Aurra appears in just one set and her minifigure is almost completely built out of unique pieces—only her arms and hands can be found on other minifigures.

Bouny Hunter Assault Gunship (set 7930)
Aurra Sing knows exactly what will fetch the highest ransom. In this set, she's managed to get hold of a LEGO Jedi holocron! Aurra's minifigure stores it in a secret chamber aboard the bounty hunter gunship.

Weapons vest
The back of Aurra's unique torso is printed with her brown vest, in which she stores compact weapons and extra ammo.

Long brown hair is tied up, out of the way

Unique hairstyle
Aurra's long, brown LEGO hair piece was specially designed for her 2011 minifigure. It fits into the stud on top of Aurra's otherwise bald head piece and flows neatly down her back.

Unique head piece is printed with Aurra's bright green eyes and confident smile

Utility belt

Aurra's orange jumpsuit is functional. It allows her to maneuver easily during combat

Unique leg pieces are printed with holsters for Aurra's twin pistols

DATA FILE

SET: 7930 Bounty Hunter Assault Gunship
YEAR: 2011
PIECES: 4
EQUIPMENT: Twin blaster pistols
VARIANTS: 1

Shahan Alama
PIRATE-TURNED-BOUNTY HUNTER

Shahan Alama was a pirate—until he was kicked out of the gang for being too nasty! Now he is a bounty hunter who works with Cad Bane. His mismatched clothing and bandana point to his former life as a pirate, but his angry temper and willingness to use a blaster on innocent people suggest a more violent minifigure. Fortunately, Shahan wreaks havoc in just one LEGO set.

DATA FILE
SET: 8128 Cad Bane's Speeder
YEAR: 2010
PIECES: 4
EQUIPMENT: Blaster
VARIANTS: 1

Dark red bandana hat piece is unique to Shahan. Hondo Ohnaka wears it in black (p.13)

Weequay skin
There are three Weequay minifigures: Shahan, Hondo Ohnaka (p.13), and Turk Falso (p.14). They all have faces printed with Weequay skin, but the patterns and colors vary between the three LEGO villains.

Shahan's unique head piece is printed with a murderous expression and a Weequay skin pattern, which continues on the back

Pearl gold arm was taken from a combat droid to replace Shahan's destroyed right arm

Protective chestplate worn around the neck

Belt was stolen from a Twi'lek nobleman

Shahan has a blaster—and is not afraid to use it!

Shahan's armor
Shahan's chestplate is printed on the back of his torso, too. Working together with Cad Bane has its risks!

Sugi

HONORABLE BOUNTY HUNTER

Bounty hunter Sugi is honest but deadly. Whether she is sent to capture a Jedi Knight or protect a family of poor farmers, she will not give up until the mission is complete. Sugi's minifigure wears functional clothes that help her get the job done. She doesn't need anything else—apart from her weapons! Sugi carries out many missions, but she only appears in one set.

DATA FILE

SET: 7930 Bounty Hunter Assault Gunship
YEAR: 2011
PIECES: 3
EQUIPMENT: Blaster, vibroblade
VARIANTS: 1

Sugi is an Iridonian Zabrak. Her head piece has small printed horns and precise face tattoos

The back of Sugi's unique head piece is printed with two more horns and Sugi's purple hair. Her hair is pulled into a neat top knot, so it doesn't get in her minifigure's way during a mission

Sugi's unique torso is printed with her simple red vest and metal necklace—her most treasured possession

Vibroblade vibrates to make it more efficient than a regular blade

Sugi's weapon of choice is an EE-3 carbine rifle

Plain gray pants give Sugi ease of movement in combat

Embo

KYUZO BOUNTY HUNTER

Embo is a Kyuzo bounty hunter with sand-green, scaly skin and yellow eyes. He is part of Sugi's team of bounty hunters on board the Bounty Hunter Assault Gunship (set 7930). His minifigure carries a bowcaster and is made up of many unique pieces, including finely detailed hat, head, torso, and leg pieces.

Multifunctional

Embo's multi-purpose hat with traditional Kyuzo markings is a 3x3 inverted radar LEGO piece. The same piece (in black, without special printing) is also used for the Imperial probe droid.

Embo's metal hat can also be thrown as a weapon or used as a shield

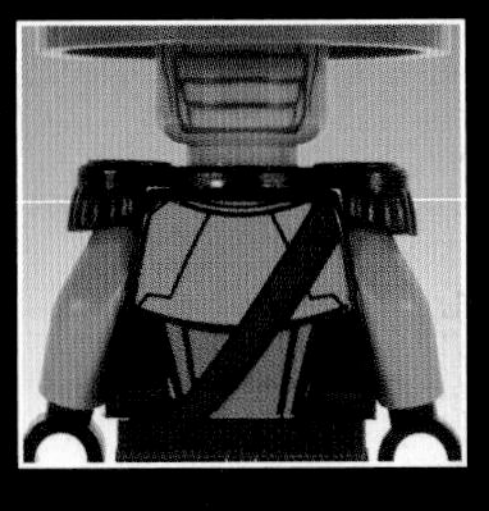

Straps and armor

The back of Embo's torso contains more printed detail, which continues the pattern of his armor and ammo belt.

Epaulets piece is also worn by Hondo Ohnaka (p.13)

Embo wears a bronze breathing mask to filter moisture out of the air

Modified bowcaster

Unique torso is printed with Embo's sturdy armor and his ammunition strap

Utility belt printed on hip piece

Unique leg piece is printed with Embo's Kyuzo-patterned wrap

DATA FILE

SET: 7930 Bounty Hunter Assault Gunship
YEAR: 2011
PIECES: 5
EQUIPMENT: Bowcaster
VARIANTS: 1

Mandalorian
ARMORED WARRIOR

The Mandalorian is a deadly soldier from the planet Mandalore. He owns many weapons, but his distinctive blue and gray armor is his most treasured possession. Appearing in only one LEGO set, the Mandalorian's minifigure joins forces with the Separatists—even though his sturdy armor was the inspiration for clone trooper armor!

Mandalorian Battle Pack (set 7914)
Four armored Mandalorian minifigures attack the clone army in this LEGO set. They are equipped with a speeder and a variety of weapons, including a blaster turret, long-range rifle, and blasters.

Helmet has similar markings to Jango Fett's helmet

DATA FILE

SET: 7914 Mandalorian Battle Pack
YEAR: 2011
PIECES: 5
EQUIPMENT: Jetpack, twin blaster pistols
VARIANTS: 1

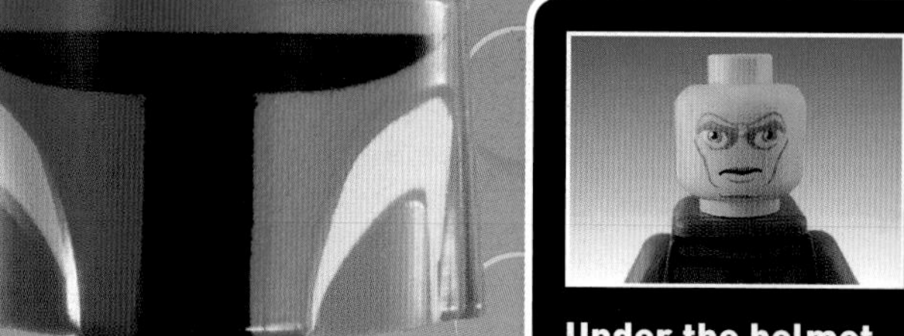

Under the helmet
Beneath the Mandalorian's helmet is a unique LEGO head piece printed with blue eyes and pale features.

Jetpack fits around minifigure's neck

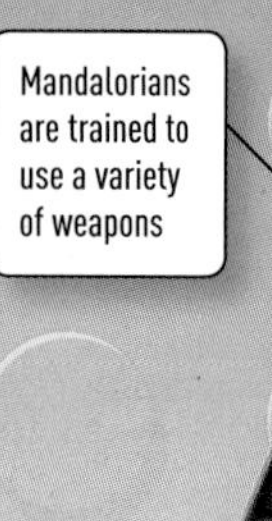

Mandalorians are trained to use a variety of weapons

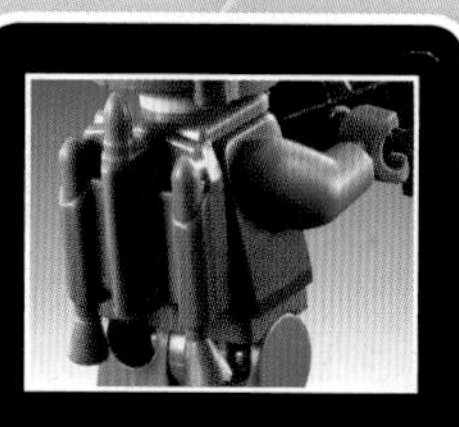

Jetpack
The Mandalorian's armor is fitted with a jetpack. Jango Fett also wears a jetpack, but it is attached to his helmet.

Mandalorian armor is famous in the LEGO *Star Wars* galaxy. It is made from an almost indestructible metal, called beskar

Mos Eisley Cantina (set 4501)
This saloon on the desert planet Tatooine has shady alcoves where secret conversations can take place unseen. Here, Han Solo and Greedo discuss the unpaid debts Han owes Jabba the Hutt. Luckily, the table they have chosen has a secret compartment for Han to hide his blaster inside!

Rodian bounty hunter Greedo is looking for Han Solo to recover money owed to his boss, Jabba the Hutt. He has caught up with Han in the Mos Espa Cantina (set 4501). But only one of them can walk out alive. A clue as to who that might be: Greedo appears in only this one LEGO *Star Wars* set!

Greedo
BOUNTY HUNTER

Large disc-shaped eyes with light reflectors

Painted elongated snout

Greedo's unique arms have painted tan stripes

First Rodian
Greedo was the first Rodian minifigure and his pimpled head-mold was designed specially for him. Greedo's fellow Rodians, Onaconda Farr and W. Wald, have since used the same head-mold but in different colors.

Tan vest over sky-blue jumpsuit

Reddish-brown hips with sky-blue legs are unique to the Greedo minifigure

DATA FILE
SET: 4501 Mos Eisley Cantina
YEAR: 2003
PIECES: 3
EQUIPMENT: None
VARIANTS: 1

IG-88
BOUNTY HUNTER

Assassin droid IG-88 stalks the LEGO *Star Wars* galaxy in three sets, and in each one he has a slightly different look—though each is as intimidating as the last. The monstrous minifigure is obsessed with hunting and killing, and he comes well equipped to pursue his passion. His round, sensor-filled head can see in all directions at once!

IG-88 has individual orange sensors on his silver head plate. Pre-2011 variants of his minifigure have a translucent orange round plate piece

Cone-shaped head has motion, sound, and heat sensors that help IG-88 catch his prey

IG-88's body is made up of identical pieces to the LEGO battle droid

One of IG-88's hands is at a 90 degree angle to his opposite hand so he can hold his blaster vertically

DATA FILE

SET: 10221 Ultimate Super Star Destroyer
YEAR: 2011
PIECES: 8
EQUIPMENT: Blaster, blaster rifle
VARIANTS: 3

STAR VARIANTS

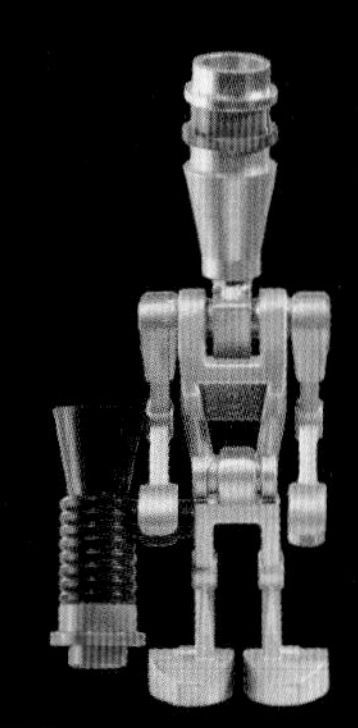

Silver assassin
This metallic silver variant of IG-88 appears in *Slave I* (set 6209), released in 2006. He carries an older version of a LEGO *Star Wars* blaster.

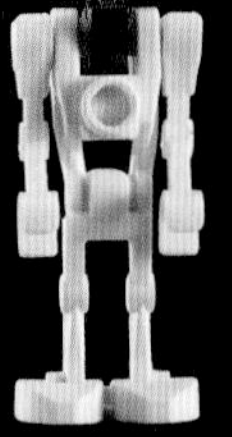

White assassin
This white droid appears on the LEGO Death Star (set 10188). He is thought to be a variant of IG-88, but he is not named as him on the set box.

Dengar
BANDAGED BOUNTY HUNTER

DATA FILE
SET: 10221 Ultimate Super Star Destroyer
YEAR: 2011
PIECES: 4
EQUIPMENT: Blaster rifle
VARIANTS: 2

This minifigure might wear makeshift armor, but don't underestimate him! Dengar is a dangerous bounty hunter. He is hired by Darth Vader to capture the *Millennium Falcon* and its passengers. Two variants of Dengar appear in two LEGO *Star Wars* sets, both with his huge Valken-38 blaster rifle close at hand.

Dengar once suffered a severe head injury. Imperial agents fixed most of the damage, but Dengar always wears a head bandage

Scarred face from a swoop-racer crash

Dengar's armor is built from discarded Imperial materials. It includes pieces of armor from sandtroopers, snowtroopers, and stormtroopers

Dengar painted his armor gray

White gloves to protect hands

STAR VARIANT

Ninja bandage
The 2006 Dengar variant comes with the LEGO set *Slave I* (set 6209). His torso and legs are different and the minifigure's standard LEGO head piece is covered with a white Ninja hood.

Bounty hunters
Most of the bounty hunters hired by Darth Vader to track down the Rebels can be found in LEGO *Star Wars* sets. IG-88, Dengar, Boba Fett, and Bossk (pp.22–25) have all been made into LEGO minifigures. Only Zuckuss and 4-LOM remain elusive.

Boba Fett
BOUNTY HUNTER

Mandalorian bounty hunter

Boba Fett appears in eight LEGO *Star Wars* sets, in six distinct variations. Boba's latest incarnation is battle-worn, but he is equipped with everything he needs to catch his prey: a probing rangefinder, a powerful jetpack, and his favorite EE-3 carbine blaster rifle.

DATA FILE

SET: 8097 *Slave I*
YEAR: 2010
PIECES: 7
EQUIPMENT: Jetpack, blaster, pauldron cloth
VARIANTS: 6

Blue-gray detachable rangefinder fits into a hole in Boba's helmet

Gray markings are battle damage

Jetpack (behind) is a sand-green version of the white jetpack used on the clone jetpack trooper

Wookiee hair is worn as a prize

Tattered fabric pauldron cloth is unique to Boba

Gray circular barrel is a Technic piece attached to a blaster gun

STAR VARIANTS

Bronze Boba
There are only two of these solid bronze Boba Fetts in existence. One was given away to a lucky competition winner as part of the LEGO "May the 4th" promotion in 2010.

Cloud City
This variant of Boba Fett has lots of detail, with printing on his arms and legs. It has only ever appeared in one LEGO *Star Wars* set—Cloud City (set 10123), released in 2003.

The man beneath
Boba never removes his helmet in public, but a peek under his LEGO helmet reveals a battle-scarred face.

Bossk
ALIEN BOUNTY HUNTER

***Slave I* (set 8097)**
Bossk helps his fellow bounty hunter Boba Fett to capture Han Solo inside a block of carbonite in this 2010 set. Bossk doesn't have a seat aboard Fett's starship, *Slave I*, but he can fit beneath the cabin during flight.

This terrifying Trandoshan bounty hunter made his minifigure debut alongside redesigns of Boba Fett and Han Solo in 2010's *Slave I* (set 8097), although he doesn't actually have a place to sit aboard the LEGO starship! Bossk's reptilian head, complete with smooth horns and sharp teeth, was specially cast for this dangerous LEGO minifigure.

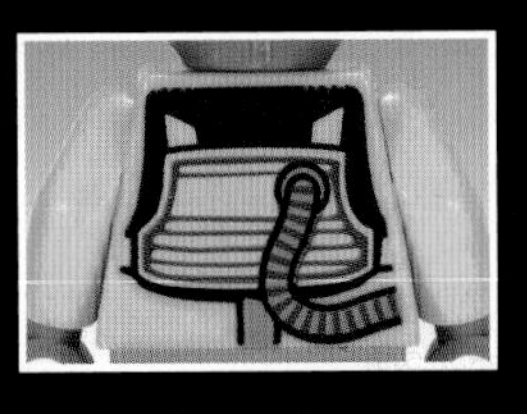

Flying in style
Bossk's flight suit has intricate details on the back as well as the front.

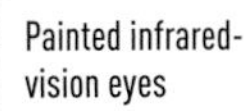

Painted infrared-vision eyes

Unique sand-green head is made from hard ABS plastic

Painted white teeth

Blaster rifle is the weapon of choice for many LEGO *Star Wars* minifigures, including assassin droids and senate commandos

White flak vest

Yellow high-altitude pressure suit

Bossk's body
The torso design on Bossk's flight suit is unique to him. It is more detailed than the flight suit sported by Rebel pilots Luke Skywalker, Biggs Darklighter, Wedge Antilles, Dutch Vander, and Dak Ralter.

DATA FILE
SET: 10221 Ultimate Super Star Destroyer
YEAR: 2011
PIECES: 3
EQUIPMENT: Blaster rifle
VARIANTS: 1

Gamorrean Guard

JABBA'S PIG GUARD

The Gamorrean guard protects Jabba the Hutt in two LEGO sets. Brutish, strong, and dull-witted, his minifigure does whatever his boss Jabba tells him and never makes a fuss. His minifigure wears sand-green armor that is attached to his unique head piece, and is armed with a deadly vibro-ax.

Vibro-ax can inflict a lethal wound with minimal effort

Gamorreans are boar-like creatures with horns and a snout

DATA FILE

SET: 6210 Jabba's Sail Barge
YEAR: 2006
PIECES: 3
EQUIPMENT: Vibro-ax
VARIANTS: 2

Head and torso armor are a single, unique piece. It fits over a plain reddish-brown LEGO torso

STAR VARIANT

Gray-armed guard
The original variant of this minifigure comes in the 2003 set Jabba's Prize (set 4476). He has gray arms, green hands, and a brown hip piece—but is just as ugly as the 2006 variant.

Turn around
The Gamorrean guard is well protected. His armor fits over the front and back of his torso.

Jabba's Sail Barge (set 6210)
The Gamorrean guard watches over Jabba's prisoners Han Solo and Luke Skywalker in this set. Little does he know that his fellow skiff guard is actually Lando Calrissian in disguise!

Bib Fortuna
TWI'LEK ASSISTANT

Jabba's Message (set 4475)
Bib Fortuna guards the entrance to Jabba's palace in this set—the only one he comes in. When R2-D2 and C-3PO turn up, Bib and the eye droid in the palace door interview the droids before they enter.

Bib Fortuna is Jabba the Hutt's eerie assistant. The Twi'lek minifigure decides who gets to speak to Jabba—and who doesn't. His rare minifigure only comes in one LEGO set, dressed in dark blue robes with a metal chestplate and black cape. His chestplate might protect him from armed intruders, but it's no good against a Jedi mind trick!

Twi'leks
Just two Twi'lek minifigures have been released in LEGO *Star Wars*: Bib Fortuna and Aayla Secura. Both Twi'leks have tentacles that clip onto a standard LEGO head piece, although Bib's are longer, because he is older.

Bib is very old, and has lived in Jabba's palace for many years. His skin in pale and wrinkled from decades without sunlight

Unique hat piece depicts Bib's bulging head and fully grown Twi'lek tentacles

Unique torso is printed with a blue belt that fastens Bib's robes

Metal chestplate protects against attacks made by Jabba's enemies

DATA FILE
SET: 4475 Jabba's Message
YEAR: 2003
PIECES: 5
EQUIPMENT: Cape
VARIANTS: 1

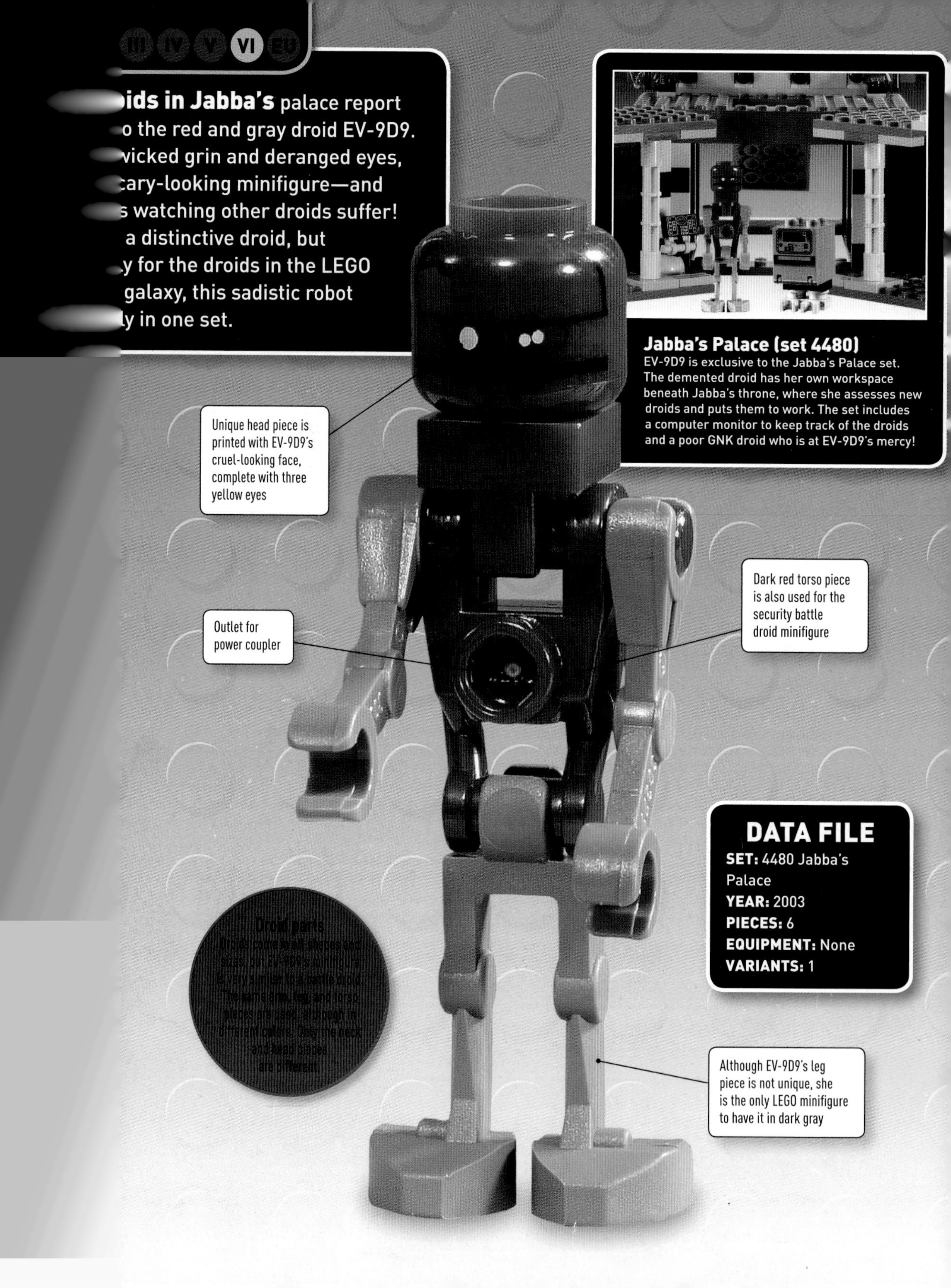

ids in Jabba's palace report
o the red and gray droid EV-9D9.
vicked grin and deranged eyes,
cary-looking minifigure—and
s watching other droids suffer!
a distinctive droid, but
y for the droids in the LEGO
galaxy, this sadistic robot
y in one set.

Jabba's Palace (set 4480)

EV-9D9 is exclusive to the Jabba's Palace set. The demented droid has her own workspace beneath Jabba's throne, where she assesses new droids and puts them to work. The set includes a computer monitor to keep track of the droids and a poor GNK droid who is at EV-9D9's mercy!

Unique head piece is printed with EV-9D9's cruel-looking face, complete with three yellow eyes

Dark red torso piece is also used for the security battle droid minifigure

Outlet for power coupler

DATA FILE

SET: 4480 Jabba's Palace
YEAR: 2003
PIECES: 6
EQUIPMENT: None
VARIANTS: 1

Droid parts
Droids come in all shapes and sizes, but EV-9D9's minifigure is very similar to a battle droid. The same arm, leg, and torso pieces are used, although in different colors. Only the neck and head pieces are different.

Although EV-9D9's leg piece is not unique, she is the only LEGO minifigure to have it in dark gray

B'omarr Monk

WALKING BRAIN

DATA FILE
SET: 4480 Jabba's Palace
YEAR: 2003
PIECES: 13
EQUIPMENT: None
VARIANTS: 1

Brain jar
The transparent jar that houses the B'omarr monk's brain is an upside-down crystal ball LEGO piece! It has appeared in various sets in the LEGO Harry Potter, LEGO Atlantis, and Fantasy Era themes.

Perhaps the strangest creatures in Jabba's palace are the B'omarr monks. These ancient beings used to be fully alive, but now only their brains remain, attached to a four-legged, spider-like droid body. The monk's minifigure is made from 13 separate pieces, and is exclusive to Jabba's Palace (set 4480).

The B'omarr monk's legs are LEGO samurai sword pieces. It is the only LEGO minifigure to feature the piece

Telepath response unit allows the monks to communicate silently with each other

Locomotion unit connects the brain support unit to the legs

Disembodied brain of the original B'omarr monk is kept alive in a fluid-filled container

Transparent orange stud piece is used as the brain

Droid legs are automated to carry the brain around Jabba's palace

LEGO crystal ball piece has a thick section of plastic at the top, which looks like a collection of fluid

Editors Hannah Dolan, Shari Last, Victoria Taylor, and Matt Jones
Designers Anne Sharples and Jon Hall
Senior Producer Lloyd Robertson
Senior DTP Designer David McDonald
Managing Editor Simon Hugo
Design Manager Guy Harvey
Creative Manager Sarah Harland
Art Director Lisa Lanzarini
Publisher Julie Ferris
Publishing Director Simon Beecroft

Additional minifigures photographed by Huw Millington, Ace Kim, Jeremy Beckett, and Tony Wood

First published in the United States in 2015
by DK Publishing
345 Hudson Street, New York, New York 10014

Contains material previously published in
LEGO® *Star Wars*® *Character Encyclopedia* (2011)

004-284485-Feb/15

A catalog record for this book is available from the Library of Congress.

ISBN: 978-5-0010-1298-6

Color reproduction by Media Development Printing Ltd, UK
Printed and bound in China

Dorling Kindersley would like to thank:
Jonathan W. Rinzler, Troy Alders, Rayne Roberts, Pablo Hidalgo, and Leland Chee at Lucasfilm; Stephanie Lawrence, Randi Sørensen, Lisbeth Langjkær, Jens Kronvold Frederiksen, Chris Bonven Johansen, and John McCormack at the LEGO Group; LEGO *Star Wars* collectors Ace Kim and Huw Millington; Emma Grange, Lisa Stock, Sarah Harland, Ellie Hallsworth, and Nicola Brown for editorial support; and Owen Bennett for design support on the cover.

www.dk.com
www.LEGO.com
www.starwars.com

A WORLD OF IDEAS:
SEE ALL THERE IS TO KNOW